THE POETRY OF ROENTGENIUM

The Poetry of Roentgenium

Walter the Educator

Silent King Books

SILENT KING BOOKS

SKB

Copyright © 2024 by Walter the Educator

All rights reserved. No part of this book may be reproduced in any manner whatsoever without written permission except in the case of brief quotations embodied in critical articles and reviews.

First Printing, 2024

Disclaimer
This book is a literary work; poems are not about specific persons, locations, situations, and/or circumstances unless mentioned in a historical context. This book is for entertainment and informational purposes only. The author and publisher offer this information without warranties expressed or implied. No matter the grounds, neither the author nor the publisher will be accountable for any losses, injuries, or other damages caused by the reader's use of this book. The use of this book acknowledges an understanding and acceptance of this disclaimer.

"Earning a degree in chemistry changed my life!"
- Walter the Educator

dedicated to all the chemistry lovers, like myself, across the world

ROENTGENIUM

A gem unveiled,

ROENTGENIUM

Roentgenium, noble yet elusive, its tale regaled.

ROENTGENIUM

Born in the fiery heart of fusion's embrace,

ROENTGENIUM

A fleeting essence in the vast cosmic space.

ROENTGENIUM

With atomic fervor, it claims its place,

ROENTGENIUM

Number one one one on the periodic race.

ROENTGENIUM

A transuranic marvel, mysterious and rare,

ROENTGENIUM

In the alchemy of stars, it's beyond compare.

ROENTGENIUM

In the forge of stars, where chaos reigns,

ROENTGENIUM

Roentgenium emerges, breaking cosmic chains.

ROENTGENIUM

Its nucleus a dance of protons and neutrons,

ROENTGENIUM

A symphony of particles, where order dawns.
ROENTGENIUM

Yet in our earthly realm, it's a transient guest,

ROENTGENIUM

A fleeting glimpse of the cosmos at its best.

ROENTGENIUM

Synthesized in laboratories, with scientific flair,

ROENTGENIUM

Unraveling mysteries, its secrets to declare.

ROENTGENIUM

In the realm of science, it beckons the bold,

ROENTGENIUM

To explore its properties, its story untold.

ROENTGENIUM

With a name that honors a pioneer's quest,

ROENTGENIUM

Roentgenium shines, put to scientific test.

ROENTGENIUM

Its electrons whirl in quantum delight,

ROENTGENIUM

A dance of energy, in the quantum night.

ROENTGENIUM

With shells of probability, they glide and spin,

ROENTGENIUM

In the quantum realm, where mysteries begin.

ROENTGENIUM

A metal of wonder, with properties unique,

ROENTGENIUM

Roentgenium's essence, a scientific clique.

ROENTGENIUM

Its bonds defy convention, its behavior arcane,

ROENTGENIUM

In the realm of chemistry, it plays a different game.

ROENTGENIUM

Catalyzing reactions with a touch so light,

ROENTGENIUM

Roentgenium whispers secrets in the night.

ROENTGENIUM

A catalyst of change, in chemical delight,

ROENTGENIUM

Its presence sparks transformations, igniting insight.
ROENTGENIUM

But like a ghost, it vanishes from sight,

ROENTGENIUM

Decaying swiftly, in the blink of light.

ROENTGENIUM

A fleeting glimpse of cosmic might,

ROENTGENIUM

Roentgenium fades into the cosmic night.

ROENTGENIUM

Yet in the annals of science, its legacy remains,

ROENTGENIUM

A testament to human curiosity's chains.

ROENTGENIUM

For in the quest for knowledge, we boldly explore,

ROENTGENIUM

The mysteries of Roentgenium, forevermore.

ROENTGENIUM

So raise a glass to this elemental star,

ROENTGENIUM

Roentgenium, in laboratories afar.

ROENTGENIUM

For in its fleeting presence, we find our place,

ROENTGENIUM

In the grand tapestry of cosmic grace.

ROENTGENIUM

ABOUT THE CREATOR

Walter the Educator is one of the pseudonyms for Walter Anderson. Formally educated in Chemistry, Business, and Education, he is an educator, an author, a diverse entrepreneur, and he is the son of a disabled war veteran. "Walter the Educator" shares his time between educating and creating. He holds interests and owns several creative projects that entertain, enlighten, enhance, and educate, hoping to inspire and motivate you.

Follow, find new works, and stay up to date with Walter the Educator™ at WaltertheEducator.com

www.ingramcontent.com/pod-product-compliance
Lightning Source LLC
LaVergne TN
LVHW012049070526
838201LV00082B/3869